ORIGINAL PAPERS

REGARDING

TRADE IN ENGLAND AND ABROAD

DRAWN UP ABOUT 1620

ORIGINAL PAPERS

REGARDING

TRADE IN ENGLAND AND ABROAD

DRAWN UP

BY

JOHN KEYMER

FOR INFORMATION OF KING JAMES I

ABOUT

1620

EDITED WITH AN INTRODUCTION

BY

M. F. LLOYD PRICHARD

AUGUSTUS M. KELLEY · PUBLISHERS
New York
1967

First Published 1967

Copyright 1967 by Augustus M. Kelley

LIBRARY OF CONGRESS CATALOGUE CARD NUMBER
67-29746

PRINTED IN THE UNITED STATES OF AMERICA
by SENTRY PRESS, NEW YORK, N. Y. 10019

CONTENTS

ACKNOWLEDGEMENTS

I have pleasure in acknowledging with thanks permission from the Edinburgh University Library and E. R. S. Fifoot, Esq., Librarian, to use the Laing MS. copy of Keymer's work.

I am also grateful to the Controller of H.M. Stationery Office for allowing me to use their MSS. of Keymer's work to check the Laing MS. and also the MSS. of Keymer's letters to Carleton (unpublished Crown Copyright material).

INTRODUCTION

In 1614, Tobias Gentleman, fisherman and mariner, published *England's Way to Win Wealth and to employ ships and mariners or A Plain Description what great profite it will bring unto the Commonwealth of England by the erecting, building and adventuring of busses to sea a-fishing. With a true relation of the inestimable wealth that is yearely taken out of His Majesties Seas by the Hollanders by their numbers of Busses, Pinkes and Lineboats . . . and also a discourse of the Sea Coast towns of England.*

The pamphlet was the result of a conference between the author and John Keymer. Gentleman says: "It was my fortune, some two years past to be sent for into the company of one Master Keymer who is a man very well deserving of his country; and he knowing me to have experience in Fisher-affairs, demanded of me the Charge both of Busses and Line-boats after the Hollanders fashion; and showed me some few notes that he had gathered and gotten from other men of my Trade which he seemed greatly to esteem; for that himself was altogether unexperienced in such Business. And further I delivered to him certain principal Notes . . . he said that he did mind to show them unto the Right Honourable Council."[1]

Gentleman denies that he has any literary ability and says that he was "more skilled in nets, lines and Hooks than in Rhetorick, Logic or Learned Books" but finding that nothing came of his scheme he decided to publish his collection himself and was encouraged to do so by a subscriber because of a complaint "which the Nation still has occasion to continue from the Dutch usurpation on our Fishery."[2]

He begins his work by describing the economic success of the Dutch who had "grown exceeding rich and strong in fortified Towns and beautiful Buildings in Plenty of money and Gold, in Trade and Traffick with all other Nations and have so increased and multiplied their Shipping and Mariners that all other Nations and Countries in the World do admire them. Moreover, whereas one Haven in one of their Towns did, in former times, contain their ships and Shipping with infinite cost, now they have cut out two Havens more to a Town

---

[1] *England's Way to Win Wealth*. See Harleian Miscellany, 1808, Volume III, pp. 378-90. The pamphlet was republished in 1660 as *The Best Way to make England the richest and wealthiest country in Europe by advancing the Fishing Trade*. See the *Dictionary of National Biography* for Professor Pollard's comment on Gentleman and also the *Dictionary of Political Economy* for Professor Palgrave's account. Palgrave says that Gentleman owed much to Keymer's investigations. Pollard says that Gentleman gave Keymer the benefit of his experience.

[2] Was this Henry, Earl of Northampton, Warden of the Cinque Ports, to whom the book was dedicated?

and at this present are all three Havens scarce sufficient with room enough to contain their ships and shipping." The Dutch had contrived to get wealthy through fishing. They had nothing growing in their own land and were compelled to fetch wood, iron, hemp, hoops and barrels, bread, corn, etc. from outside. He ended by giving a detailed description of the ports of England and says that he would have set down the particular numbers of and the total sum gained by the fishermen if he had been commanded but would content himself merely with saying that there were o-o barks, o-o boats, having o-o men apiece, amounting to the sum of o-o (sic).

In fact, Keymer was not so ignorant as Gentleman suggests for he had already written in 1601 a pamphlet addressed to Queen Elizabeth entitled *Observations made upon the Dutch fishing.*[3] The purpose of the pamphlet was to argue that there was more wealth raised from herrings and other fish in Her Majesty's seas by neighbouring nations in one year than the King of Spain had from the Indies in four and also that there were 20,000 ships and other vessels and about 400,000 people set to work by sea and land and maintained solely

---

[3] The MS. was believed to be in the Goldsmiths' Library, London, but it is not there now. It was printed in 1664 by order of the Lord Mayor and edited by Sir Edward Ford. (But *Dutch Policy,* 1764, gives the date of the first print as 1604.) It was reissued in English in the *Phoenix,* 1707, No. 8 in Volume I of *A Collection of Choice Tracts,* 1721, and in *A Small Collection of valuable tracts relating to the Herring Fishery,* 1751. It was published in Germany in Part XII of the *Diarium Europaeum,* Frankfurt, 1660.

by fishing upon the coasts of England, Scotland and Ireland.

Keymer says that, desiring to get knowledge for his country's good, he travelled in France, Germany and other countries and made discoveries relating to the rapid rise of ship owning in Holland. He declares that that country which was not so big as one of the English counties (18 Dutch Miles long and 5 broad) had about it 30 walled towns, 400 villages and 20,000 sail of ship and hoy which was more than England, France, Spain, Portugal, Italy, Scotland, Denmark, Poland, Sweden and Russia possessed put together and furthermore Holland built every year 1000 new ships, "having in their soil neither matter to build nor merchandizes to set them forth."

Keymer then describes the type of boat owned by the Hollanders. They had about 4,100 fishing ships and vessels "whereof 100 Dogger-boats, 700 Pinks and Well-boats, 700 Strand-boxes, 400 evers and 400 Galliots, Drivers and Todboats and 1200 busses."[4] He says that since he had urged the building of 200 busses for England, the Hollanders had made 800 more. The 1500 strand boats, evers, galliots, drivers and todboats were built on their own coasts and every one of them set on

---

[4] Dogger-boat = two masted fishing smack; pink = pingk, a vessel with a narrow stern; well-boat = a fishing-boat with a well in its hold; galliot = a ship carrying a main mast, a mizzen-mast and a large gaff-mainsail; driver = a square-rigged vessel; buss = a two-masted herring lugger.

work one other vessel to fetch salt and to transport fish into other countries. There were therefore 3000 vessels and 40,000 persons employed and maintained by fishing upon their own coasts. The pinks and well-boats were about 60 to 100 tuns apiece, the dogger boats about 150 tuns and these fished on the coasts of England and Scotland for cod and ling and these also set to work one other vessel to fetch salt and carry the fish into other countries. The busses were from 60 to 200 tuns apiece and were used to take herrings from Baughamless in Scotland down the coasts of England to the mouth of the Thames from June to November,[5] and a great buss took 8 to 20 lasts of herrings in one night and 40 to 100 lasts were transported back to Holland. But, says, Keymer, the English contented themselves with fishing for seven weeks only with small crayets and cobles from 5 to 20 tuns apiece and took 1 to 3 lasts a night and if 7 were brought home it was considered wonderful. Moreover, he says, the English stayed until the herrings came right up to the coast and sometimes allowed them to pass by before they bothered to look "and so they lost God's blessing." Often, he adds, they spent all their gains in

---

[5] Cf. *Anglo-Dutch Rivalry* by Rev. George Edmundson, 1911, p. 160, where it is stated that the Dutch fishing fleet was accustomed to sail for Scottish waters between the Shetlands and Cape Buchan Ness in the Middle of June, ending up at the mouth of the Thames in November where they fished to the end of the year and the beginning of the next.

the alehouses until they were driven back to sea by debt.[6]

The Hollanders also used 400 other ships called Gaynes and Evers to take herrings at Yarmouth where they were sold for ready money. They had also 800 other ships trading every year to London with cod and ling taken in English seas and, having sold them, they carried away fine gold which was made into base gold in their own country. All this, he says, was "a great hurt to the wealth and strength of our land and hindrance to Navigation and Mariners and employment of the poor of this nation." The Hollanders had also inflicted damage by enacting a law that the English should sell no white herrings or any other fish in Holland. In twenty-six weeks the Hollanders took over 300,000 lasts (12 barrels to the last) and since these were sold to the merchants at £10 or £12 a last, they gained £3,600,000. Their merchants sent them all over Europe where they sold from £16 to £36 a last and thus gained about £5,000,000. Thousands of people shared in these gains because they put money into the busses and therefore young people were wealthy even before they married. With the money obtained from selling fish, they bought goods with which they

---

[6] Cf. *Empire of the North Atlantic* by Gerald S. Graham, 1958, for an account of the successful appropriation by the Dutch of the herring fisheries. Graham quotes figures from Pahl's *Die Kolonialpolitik Richelieus* based on calculations from E. Baasch, *Hollandische Wirtschaftgesichte*, to show that by 1610 Holland controlled about 3000 merchant ships along with 3000 fishing craft. He notes too that the Dutch experimented with shipbuilding and that the "buss" represented a significant break with the older traditions (pp. 24-26).

traded also and thus the country profited. Customs dues added to its wealth and the people were wealthy though they had little growing in their country. The number of ships and mariners had increased. Every town had been improved with sumptuous buildings and where they formerly had but one haven in a town they now had two or three "and yet not able to hold their ships if they were all at home at one time."[7]

To prove his point that considerable employment was found through the fishing industry, Keymer says: "One buss of 100 or 80 tuns employeth three ships, sets on work and maintaineth both at sea and land above 400 persons and 30 several trades and occupations; it may evidently appear how the 1,000 sail of pinks, well-boats and doggerboats and their 2,000 great busses do set on work 200,000 Persons and 7,200 sail of ships of the Hollanders by fishing upon Her Majesty's coasts. First, she sets on work in her own Hull within her self of Mariners and Fishermen 40. Secondly, she imployeth three ships besides her self, one to fetch home salt into their own country, another to carry forth barrels and salt into her at sea and to bring her Herrings back into her own country and the third to transport her Herrings beyond the Seas; and in three ships and Busses 100 Mariners are employed. Thus are three ships and 100 persons busied at

[7] Cf. Gentleman's comment. The co-operative enterprise or Rederij by which people joined together to buy, own, build, charter or freight a ship and its cargo is described by C. R. Boxer. *The Dutch Seaborne Empire 1600-1800*, 1965, p. 6.

sea by one Buss. Thirdly, at Land of spinners and Hemp-winders to make Cables and Cordage, likewise Yarn twine and thread for the making of nets and sails, Saltmen to make Salt upon Salt, Coopers in great abundance to make Barrels, Block and Bowl-makers for ships, Porters, Keelmen, Lightermen and Labourers to be imployed in carrying and removing; as also Hewers and Squarers of Timber, Sawyers of Planks, Carpenters, Shipwrights, Smiths, Pledgmen, Carmen, Boatmen, Brewers, Bakers and a number of other persons too tedious to repeat. The Sailsmen and the Mariners with divers others, depending upon this unsearchable business, there cannot be less than 200. So that with the former there are 300 Persons and three ships set on work by one Buss. And yet besides all these that work they have their wives, Children and Families hardly to be numbered that neither do nor can work and yet are maintained and live wealthily out of this one Buss; the Merchants, Sailsmen, Owners of Ships, Master, Mariners and Fishermen cannot deny this."

Keymer argues that fishing was more valuable to the kingdom than mining or cloth manufacturing because (1) of its effect upon the number of ships and mariners, (2) it would bring in great wealth which would make all nations "vail the bonnet to England," (3) it would provide employment and (4) the plentiful fish collected would fill the storehouses.

*   *   *   *

In 1859 McCulloch published *A Select Collection of Scarce and Valuable Tracts on Commerce* in which he included *Observations touching Trade and Commerce with the Hollander and other Nations presented to King James by Sir Walter Ralegh Knt. wherein is proved that on sea and land commodities serve to inrich and strengthen other countries against our own.* This was taken from Ralegh's *Miscellaneous Works,* 1751, but McCulloch doubts—and it seems rightly—that Ralegh was the author. He notes that William Oldys in his *Life of Ralegh* (1829) attributed it to John Keymer who already had written his *Observations on the Dutch Fishery* in or about the year 1601.

An examination of the second work shows it to have many arguments and expressions in common with the earlier work though, as Oldys comments, Ralegh had touched lightly on the same topics. But, Oldys says, no treatise of Ralegh had descended into such minute examples and calculations and he adds that having seen several MSS. of the second work in the libraries of the nobility and gentry and compared them with the MS. of the first work "written also in the little old neat hand," he was bound to conclude that "whoever has read these two pieces will allow that one hand writ them."[8]

Oldys believes Keymer to have been a vintner who

---

[8] *The Life of Sir Walter Ralegh* by William Oldys, 1829, Volume I, pp. 441 following. Note that Edmundson, *op. cit.*, considered the work to be by Ralegh and dated its presentation about 1610.

Ralegh many years before had licensed to retail wine in Cambridge and about whom Ralegh had been involved in a controversy with the University in that town. The story is of interest not only because of its relevancy to Keymer but because the University still possesses the extraordinary privilege which enabled it nearly four hundred years ago to engage Ralegh in conflict.

In 1584, at the same time that Elizabeth gave Ralegh the patent for the discovering of remote countries she gave him another to license the vending of wines from the profits of which he could support his voyages of discovery. Ralegh thereupon licensed John Keymer to sell wine in Cambridge. The University, however, possessed the right to license vintners in the town, a privilege given them in Richard II's reign according to the Vice-Chancellor and Ralegh's action was deemed an invasion of their right. In June, the Vice-Chancellor and the Heads of the Colleges addressed a letter to Lord Burghley asking him to influence Ralegh to withdraw the license from Keymer, reminding him that two years previously the townspeople had made an unsuccessful attempt to license vintners. They also wrote to the Earl of Leicester asking him to speak to Ralegh on their behalf.

Ralegh made the suggestion that the question should be referred to Counsel but this was refused. Scholars of Cambridge University and Baxter, "an esquire beadle,"

licensed by the University to sell wine, "opposed Keymer and his wife with such violence that she was likely
to have died."[9] Keymer complained to Ralegh who
wrote to the Vice-Chancellor and the rest of the Masters
to tell them how offended he was by this disregard of the
Queen's grant. He threatened that if Keymer was not
permitted to enjoy his license he would take steps to
protect him in it. He was sure, however, that the offend-
ers would be punished and ended this first letter of 9th
July 1584 "Your very affectionate loving friend."

After seven months' silence, Ralegh wrote again after
learning that Keymer had been summoned to appear
before the Vice-Chancellor and the Heads of the Colleges and been committed to prison. Ralegh expressed
surprise at what he called "their peremptory and proud
manner of dealing"[10] and declared that he would pursue
the matter of his patent further, ending this letter "Your
friend as you shall give cause."

The Vice-Chancellor sent an account of the proceedings against Keymer to Lord Burghley, telling him that
he had sent proctors to restrain Keymer from selling
wine. Keymer insisted on his right and the Beadle and
proctors, therefore, pulled Keymer's sign down. Keymer
restored it to position and the following day, the University authorities went again to pull it down but were

---

[9] Oldys, *op. cit.*

[10] See *Annals of Cambridge* by C. H. Cooper, p. 398.

met with boiling water mixed with lime and ashes and with stones. The sign stayed up.[11] The matter was referred to the King's Bench.

The Vice-Chancellor wrote also "a handsome apologetical letter" to Ralegh "setting forth that the hard opinion he had conceived of them for this matter, made them doubt what manner of answer they might address to him without offence; and that their silence was so ill taken, they knew not how their endeavours to excuse it might give him satisfaction. That they had not neglected means to procure his favour for the quiet enjoyment of that whereof they had fruition for above two hundred years; not omitted to become petitioners to him in a very humble manner. That his counsel had not made any just exception against their charters; and those who had the hearing of the case thought them to have the better warrant. Yet that he used such hard terms as they little looked for at his hands; being by birth a gentleman; by education trained up to the knowledge of good letters; instructed with the liberal disposition of a university, the foundation and nursery of all humanity; and further by God's good blessing advanced in court from whence the very name of courtesy is drawn."[12] The Vice-Chancellor

---

[11] Cooper, *op. cit.* The assistant to the Keeper of the University of Cambridge archives informs me that the Act Books of the Vice-Chancellor's Court at that date are incomplete and no record remains of the Keymer case. Cooper got his material from other sources (manuscript and printed).

[12] Oldys, *op. cit.*

pointed out that Ralegh had got his title by the Queen's prerogative. Their charters were based on the same "and as he would think it hard to have his patent impeached by an after-grant, they hoped he would with like equity measure them who were warranted to have the sole dealing with all vintners in Cambridge town and the precincts thereof."[13] He asked Ralegh to respect their privileges so that they might be left in no worse state for posterity. The explanation was added that Keymer had been imprisoned for failing to appear before the judge when ordered.

In July 1585, Burghley sent the opinion of the two chief justices, Sir Christopher Wraye and Sir Edmund Anderson, which was that "Mr. Rawlie" could nominate no vintners in Cambridge because that privilege belonged to the University by usage and charters from Her Majesty, confirmed by Parliament. It seems, however, that Keymer continued to trade because Leicester in 1586 wrote again to the Vice-Chancellor stating that he must be stopped. After this, no more is heard. But it may be that Ralegh befriended Keymer further and the latter might have learnt of Ralegh's views, particularly on shipping, when he lamented that "strangers should be permitted to eat us out, by exporting both our own commodities and those of foreign nations." Keymer went on to make the close examination of England's position vis-

13 *Ibid.*

à-vis countries like Holland from which came the pamphlet written in 1601.

*   *   *   *

A comparison of the earlier pamphlet with the later one shows many resemblances. The same comments are made about the size and multiplier effect of the great sea business of fishing. Thus, in the first, it is stated that "it is most evidently true that His Majesty's seas are far richer than the King of Spain's Indies and there is more made of Fish taken by the French, Biscainers, Portuguese, Spaniards, Hollanders, Hamburghers, Bremers, Embdeners, Scotish, Irish and English in one year than the King of Spain hath in four years out of the Indies. For there are about 20,000 ships and vessels and about 400,000 Persons set on work and maintained only by the Fishing upon the Coasts of England, Scotland and Ireland." It is also stated that Holland had about it 20,000 sail of ship, more than ten other countries put together and later a list of 4,100 fishing ships, divided up in categories is given. The second pamphlet, in the section Touching Fishinge, says that "Fishing doth imploye neere 20,000 ships and vessels" and again refers to the 400,000 people employed thereby and credits the Hollanders with 3,000 fishing vessels and 9,000 other ships and vessels given employment and 150,000 persons more to dress and transport fish and bring back goods so that they were able to build 1,000 ships each year "havinge not one tymber tree growing in theire own countries nor home bred commodities to layde 100 ships and yet they have 20,000 ships and vessels and all imployed."

Such comments on the herring fishery and the size of the fleet owned by the Hollanders must have carried weight, as McCulloch notes, in winning over public opinion in England to projects for improving fisheries. The judicious observations on the circumstances which helped to make the Hollanders wealthy must also have had their influence. The explanation that they piled up riches through their sobriety and industry is one frequently repeated in early seventeenth century literature.

The second pamphlet is, however, much more than a reminder of the potential value of the fishing industry. In addition to the emphasis placed on "the wonderful imployment of theire busses for fishinge and the greate returnes they make," Keymer gives other reasons for the superior wealth and strength of the Hollanders. For example, they were astute in storing grain. This was done by the Merchant Staplers and he says that Amsterdam was never without 700,000 quarters of corn, "besides the plentie they daylie vent." Therefore, when there was a dearth in other countries, Holland and the other "petty states" benefited. But more important still was the institution of free or relatively free trade. "The libertie of free traffique for strangers to buy and sell in Holland . . . maketh great entercourse . . . the small duties leavyed

upon merchants draweth all nations to trade with them
. . . theire giving free Custome inwardes and outwardes
for any new erected trade by means whereof they have
already gotten almost the sole trade into theire own
handes." Other nations also levied small customs on in-
coming goods but the Hollanders' rates were spectacu-
larly low as compared with the English exactions and
Holland benefited nevertheless because of the multitude
of commodities attracted to it.[14]

This emphasis on low customs duties and freer trade
is noteworthy. Keymer ranks amongst the earliest advo-
cates of free trade.

The second pamphlet carries also additional material
on the subject of credit and overtrading on credit and
undervaluing of the English coinage in relation to con-
tinental countries and, most interesting of all, a discus-
sion of the woollen cloth trade.

Keymer told Gentleman about 1612 that he intended
to show his notes "unto the Right Honourable Council." He may have done so but we learn from the second
pamphlet in the dedication to James I that he had presented an earlier work to him about fourteen or fifteen
years earlier. Oldys says that if this was done "in the

---

[14] Schumpeter in his *History of Economic Analysis* (1954) missed
Keymer's advocacy of free trade. He states that up to and after
1600, "Free Trade as a program" meant fettering or even breaking
up the merchants' companies . . . "a sort of trust busting" but
clearly Keymer went further than that.

very first year of the king's being in England, then this second must have been presented in 1617 or 1618." The Laing copy from which we have taken a transcript is headed Original Papers regarding trade in England and abroad drawn up by John Keymer for information of King James I about 1620. The Public Record Office copy ends: "Mr. Keymer discourse presented to his Maty" and is dated 1620.[15] The Calendar of State Papers (Domestic) for 1619 to 1623 lists amongst the *Undated papers 1620?* (page 208) a *"Tract by John Keymer addressed to the King*, on the importance of encouraging manufacturers in England and of increasing commerce by reduction of customs etc. showing the advantages possessed by foreign nations over the English in these and other respects, in spite of the natural advantages of England; with suggestions for remedy."[16]

Keymer's arguments about the cloth trade hark back, however, to the period 1612 to 1614. He refers to a total of 80,000 undrest undyed clothes yearly transported and he comments that the undrest undyed clothes were sold to strangers who dressed, dyed and stretched them to unreasonable lengths contrary to English law

---

[15] SP 14/118. There are two copies in the Office, one without the introduction and both carry the date 1620. McCulloch's transcript is from Oldys' collection of Ralegh's works which appears to have included the P.R.O. MS. without the introduction. The Historical Manuscripts Commission's Report on the Laing Mss. gives 1620 as the date (Vol. I, p. 156).

[16] And on page 209 the second copy without the introduction is noted.

with the result that they hindered the English markets and discredited English clothiers. The kingdom lost some £400,000 through this business. The Merchant Adventurers were named the chief culprits.

It was of course between 1612 and 1614 that the campaign waged by Alderman Cockayne, supported by representatives of rival companies, against the Merchant Adventurers reached its peak. In the autumn of 1613 a special committee appointed to enquire into the business of finishing cloth reported that existing conditions meant great loss of employment for many thousands of poor workmen and that most of the trading companies had cause to complain. For, as things were, "those clothes which for the private lucre of some fewe are transported rough and undrest are so abused by strangers that . . . they have not onelye discredited that rich commoditye of our kingdom but by the unconscionable gayne which they rayse by stretching of each cloth eight or ten yards, have greatlie discouraged all our merchants who· trade in dressed and dyed clothes and in short time will drive them altogether from their vent at their usuall places for sale."[17] The figure of 80,000 is the same as that given by Sir Julius Caesar in his notes of the Privy Council meetings in July 1614[18] and it is of interest to note that the

[17] See *Alderman Cockayne's Project and the Cloth Trade* by Astrid Friis, 1927, pp. 242-243.

[18] *Ibid.*, pp. 460-461. The author gives the impression that the same total was registered in 1612.

Merchant Adventurers, contesting Cockayne's case, left it to the "Conselors of State, whether for the hope of £300,000 a year in gaine, so great a calamity as this cause will succeeding may bring, shall be ventured upon at this time."[19]

From 1614 to 1616 was made the calamitous experiment with the new company which took over the privileges of the Merchant Adventurers and which attempted to send out dyed and dressed Cloths instead of white cloths formerly sent. The Netherlands promptly retaliated by forbidding the import of dyed cloths. The English woollen trade suffered such severe losses that by 1617 James I was forced to restore the charter of Merchant Adventurers.

It appears that Keymer was well versed in the details of the struggle and his pamphlet seems to have been written about the same time as the decision made to prohibit the export of unfinished cloth—that is, about the middle of 1614 or later the same year.[20] He sets out the arguments in favour of the "full manufactorie or our home bred commodities." At the close of his pamphlet he lists five propositions for the consideration of the king. Firstly, the appointment of a State Merchant to organise trade; secondly, the promotion of fishing; thirdly the export of coal but in English ships only; fourthly the re-

[19] *Ibid.*, p. 462. See also Coke's arguments pp. 246-247.
[20] References in Keymer's text itself point to the same conclusion; e.g., comment on the harvest failure of 1608; raising the value of gold. See footnotes.

valuation of the coinage and, lastly, the full manufacture of the native goods. Keymer asks the king to give him leave to nominate commissioners who would report to His Majesty on the best means of promoting trade and manufacture.

Keymer's pamphlet may actually have been presented to the king in 1620 for we find him making another attempt in 1622 to get the Crown interested in his proposals. On December 20, it is recorded:[21] "Commission to Charles, Prince of Wales, John Bishop of Lincoln, Lord Keeper of the Great Seal Lewis Duke of Lenox, Geo. Marquis of Buckingham, to hear the propositions which shall be made by John Keymer and to consider whether they will tend to the good of the king and commonwealth as is pretended."

Nothing came of this venture but it is of interest to find him persisting in his efforts to achieve the reforms outlined in his pamphlet. The issues he raised were still vital but by 1623 circumstances had changed somewhat, as will be shown.

In 1617 when James I had been compelled to return their charter to the Merchant Adventurers, he was naturally incensed against the Hollanders against whom he wanted to take retaliatory measures for their action over imported dressed cloth and an attempt was made to strike at them through their fishing activity on the coasts of

---

[21] Public Record Office S.P. 14/141.

his kingdom. A bitter dispute developed when tolls were levied on foreign fishermen fishing off the Scottish coast. Another cause for dispute lay in the rivalry between the Dutch and English East India Companies trading for spice in the Indies. Sir Dudley Carleton,[22] England's ambassador at the Hague, was instrumental in getting a deputation sent to London in December 1618 to discuss the points of difference between the two nations—the herring fishery, the dressed cloth question and the spice trade. Little was accomplished, however, and the deputies returned to Holland in August 1619. A further deputation arrived in 1621 but returned in April with nothing accomplished. Meantime the Merchant Adventurers were successful in transferring their court from Middleburg to Delft. They had been trying to do this for some time and eventually it was Carleton who obtained the king's consent and brought the matter to this successful conclusion, despite the persisting hostility between England and Holland. Another delegation arrived in London at the end of 1621 to discuss once again the three important questions, but although meetings were held throughout 1622, both with the Privy Council and the king, again little was achieved and the delegation returned to the Netherlands in February 1623. About this time

---

[22] Sir Dudley Carleton, Viscount Dorchester, 1573-1632, was ambassador to Venice 1610-1615, at The Hague 1616-1625, Envoy to Paris 1626, M.P. for Hastings 1626, created Baron Carleton of Imbercourt 1629, special envoy to The Hague 1626-1628, created Viscount Dorchester 1628 and Secretary of State 1628.

Prince Charles, accompanied by Buckingham, went to Madrid to enter into negotiations for his Spanish marriage. The prospect filled the Netherlands with alarm and fresh attempts were made to conciliate the English. Another delegation arrived in London in February 1624. By this time, hopes for a Spanish alliance had collapsed and the Dutch concluded a treaty of alliance in the middle of the year. Fresh negotiations opened on the subject of the long-standing disputes but these again made little progress and James I died early in 1625.[23]

Thus, from 1618 to the times of James I's death, efforts were being made to settle the differences between England and Holland and, had they succeeded, two of the major questions raised by Keymer would have been settled (i.e. the dressed cloth trade and the herring fishery). It is of further interest to find Keymer in correspondence with Sir Dudley Carleton in 1619 and it is tempting to envisage him on the periphery, at any rate, of the events of that time. The first letter[24] sent in April 1619 runs as follows:

"My very good Lord,

Finding fit means by Mr Albory that is of my old acquaintance, out of true love I could not omit to com-

---

[23] See Edmundson, *op. cit.*, Chs. 2 and 3.

[24] Public Record Office SP 14/108:17. I have put the letters in modern language. These letters do not appear in the book *The Letters from and to Sir Dudley Carleton Knt. during his embassy in Holland from January 1615/16 to December 1620*. Third Edition, 1780.

mend my service unto you, and hereby to let your Lordship understand that last Maundy Thursday, I being alone with the Secretary Manton in supper time, he received a packet from you which he read incontinently and then broke forth into these words. I hold Sir Dudley Carleton for the absolutest and sufficientist Minister to the State that is employed abroad in His Majesty's service. But I doubt he is discouraged now he hath missed the late advancement which he deserved. Whereupon I required his Honour to labour his Majesty for your good, suggesting I thought a great part of your entertainment was eaten out by interest before you could receive your means. He said, I believe that is true. I replied, A course might be taken to cure that malady if His Majesty were moved to bestow on him the creating of an Earl or a Baron: which might advance him 10,000 pounds and not exhaust one penny extraordinary out of the King's purse. And in the interim your Honour may procure him his own monies in due time. It is good, said Mr Secretary, I would he had it. Whereby I perceived his inward affection to your Lordship. That may (if you be so pleased) make use thereof. I protest, it proceedeth only out of my loyal and unfeigned love to your Lordship in whose bosom (I humbly pray) it may be interred and not be discovered as from me unto Mr. Secretary or any other, for I never opened myself in this subject to any other living creature. But I am now assured of his Honour's entire affection unto your Lordship if your wisdom shall see good to make use of him for the accomplishment thereof and advertise Mr Locke of the proceedings therein as occasion shall permit. And thus I conclude but I am and will remain ready at your Lordship's commands.

John Keymer.

London this 5th of April 1619.

Postscript. I knowing that this bearer is seriously commended to your Lordship by Mr Secretary do suppose my poor recommendations are needless. Yet because I have been long acquainted with the man whose honesty and loyalty hath been employed in affairs of good consequence for the State as Mr Trumball[25] hath experimented. In regard of his troublesome suits I cannot let to cast my mite into the treasury of your honourable furtherance unto those your friends which may there advance the efforts of his long suits for whom I am bold seriously to intercede unto your Lordship.

John Keymer.

To the right Honourable Sir Dudley Carleton Knight Lord Ambassador his Majesty of Great Britain with the States of the United Provinces at The Hague.

[In another hand: Mr Keymer the 5th of April received the 10th 1619.]

The second letter[26] sent in May 1619 runs:

Sir,

I have received two letters from you. One of them Mr Lock gave it me to the intent to take some time to show to Mr Secretary for he told me it was your will and desire that I should do it. And finding such an opportunity walking in St. James' Park, he taking an occasion to speak of a book which he showed me in his chamber touching the Hollanders' proceedings in the East Indies sent from you which he was well pleased with and gave such commendations of your carefulness and diligence that even

---

[25] Is this William Trumbull? (Diplomatist, resident in the Netherlands 1609-1625.)

[26] Public Record Office SP 14/109:58.

then I took a good time to deliver your letter; which when he had read it, he took it passing well and said he would keep it by him and so put it up in his hose and when I began to converse with him about it, his answer was that he would be mindful. But by reason of my good friend Sir William Cocken[27] (who Mr Secretary loveth well) hath some good cause to use your Honour's help. I would not have written as yet but I doubt not but that your next letter which you have from your man Locke or from me will be to good purpose touching your business. In the meantime I humbly pray you to give your best assistance to your good friends there touching Sir William Cocking's cause of suit who hath appealed to The Hague from whence it was brought to Middleburgh and now brought to The Hague again by reason of the ill justice he received at the said Middleburgh, touching your cause Sir William Cockines Councillor or Solicitor (as I command) will relate to your Honour at large. Thus being assured of your Honour's best furtherance I humbly take my leave.

Your Honour's in all true heartiness

John Keymer

London the 29th May 1619.
[Addressed to Carleton as before.]

The third letter[28] sent in July 1619 is as follows:
Right Honourable,
Understanding my good friend Mr Heather[29] to be going for Holland and by reason of sickness and other

---

[27] Is this Alderman Cockayne who was knighted in 1614?

[28] Public Record Office SP 14/109:169.

[29] Is this one of the Heathers complained of by the Merchant Adventurers as interlopers? The Company asked for a bond from them in 1618 of £1000 that they would not meddle in trade and John Heather protesting asked to be admitted to the Company.

extraordinary occasions have befallen me so as Mr Secretary and I have not been often together as before hath been the cause I have not writ unto you not put in mind of your business which he so well like when I gave him the letter you sent by Mr Locke. But now (God be thanked) I being well and my business brought to good pass I shall endeavour my selfe to do you the best offices and services shall lie in me to be done, nothing doubting but that the business you have wrote about or one other better than it, both for your honour and profit will be brought to pass before His Majesty's progresses. There is speech of a Treasurer and a Secretary which being resolved upon I am assured of your advancement. I understand not of this from Mr Secretary but by one that knoweth much in their affairs but now being to go to Mr Secretary I make account I shall know further of the business and send you word by the next. And with my humble request, that if this bearer Mr Heather have occasion to use your help in his honest cause, that you will bestead him. I humbly take my leave ever resting and remaining

Your Lordship's in all duty to be commanded

John Keymer.

Postscript. I was loath to write so much of this secret business till I had spoken with the Secretary but that I found this bearer of departure.

John Keymer

[Addressed to Carleton as before.] 1619 July 17
[In another hand: Mr Keymer the 27th of July 1619.]

Keymer appeared in these letters to be on fairly familiar terms with Carleton. The latter's desire to get advancement is well known but whether Keymer had any real influence at Court is not known. Carleton eventually rose to be Viscount Dorchester and a Secretary of State but perhaps by 1628 when this happened Keymer had died[30] for after the announcement of a commission to the Prince of Wales and the others named in 1622 to hear his propositions nothing more is heard of him. His written work remains of value primarily because of his enlightened attitude towards the possibility of freer trade between countries,[31] of his recognition of the means whereby the Dutch rose to economic supremacy, of the importance he attached — however exaggerated—to the multiplier effects of the fishing industry on employment in general.

M. F. LLOYD PRICHARD,
Associate-Professor in Economic History,
Department of Economics,
University of Auckland, New Zealand.

---

[30] If Oldys was right and the Keymer of the pamphlets is the same as the one licensed by Ralegh in 1584, by 1622 he might have been over sixty years of age if he was only in the early twenties when he became a vintner.

[31] Cf. The Supplement to the *Dictionary of National Biography* (which gives Keymer—floruit 1610-20) for a comment on Keymer as an early advocate of the need to reduce customs duties.

ORIGINAL PAPERS REGARDING
TRADE IN ENGLAND AND ABROAD
DRAWN UP BY JOHN KEYMER FOR INFORMATION OF
KING JAMES I ABOUT 1620[1]

ON TRADE — Policies of State practised in divers king-
doms for encrease of trading and trafique beyond the seas
and in England, proving that English Seas and lande Commodities doe serve to encite and strengthen other Countryes
against our owne and how to redress the same.

Observations for your most excellent Matie touching
trade and trafique beyond the seas and in England wherein
he certainly findeth that your Sea and land commodities do
serve to inrich and strengthen other Countries against your
kingdom which were the urgent causes why he endeavoured
himself to take extraordinarie paines for the redresse soe it
may stand with your majesties good likinge.

Maie it please your most excellent Matie.

According to my dutie I am imbouldened to put your
Matie in mynde that about 14 or 15 years past I presented
you a booke of such extraordinarie importance for honor
and proffitt of your Matie and posteritie and doubtinge that
it hath been layde asside and not considered of, I am in-
couraged (under your Maties pardon) to present unto you
once more, Consisting of five propositions, neither are they
grounded upon vayne or idle grounds but upon the fruition
of those wonderful blessings wherewith God hath endued
your Matie sea and land. By which measure you maie not
only inrich and fill your coffers, but also increase such
might and strength (as shall appeare if it may stand with
your Maties good likinge to put the same in execution in the
tru and right forme) soe that there is noe doubt but will

---

[1] From the Laing MS. 1152. Edinburgh University Library.

make you in short tyme a prince of so greate power as shall
make all the princes your neighbours as well glad of your
friendship as fearefull to offend you. That this is so, I
humblie desire that your Matie will vouchsafe to peruse this
advertisement with the care and judgment which God hath
given you.

Most humblie prayinge your Matie that whereas I presented these five propositions together as in their owne
natures joyntly dependinge one of another and soe linked
together as the distraction of any one will be an apparent
mayme and disablinge to the rest. That your Matie would
be pleased that they may not be separated but all handled
together joyntly and severally by Commissioners with as
much speed and secrecy as can be and made fitt to be reported to your Matie whereby I may be the better able to
performe unto your highness that which I have promised
and (by God's help) will performe upon my life, if, I be
not prevented by some that may seeke to hinder the honor
and proffitt of your Matie for their owne private endes.

The true Ground course and forme herein mentioned
shall appeare how other countries make themselves powerful and rich in all kyndes by Marchandize, Manufacture
and fulness of trade, having no commodities in their own
countries growing to do it withall.

And herein likewise shall appeare how easye it is to drawe
the wealth and strength of other countries to your kingdome, and what royall rich and plentifull meanes God hath
given this land to do it (which cannot be denyed) for support of traffique and continuall imployment of your people
for replenishinge of your Maties coffers.

And if I were not fully assured to improve your native
commodities (with other traffique) three millions of pounds

more yearly than now they are, and to bringe, not only to your Maties coffers within the space of one or three years neare two millions of poundes but to increase your revenues many thousands yearly and to please and greatly proffitt your people, I would not have undertaken soe greate a worke. All which will growe by the advancement of all kynde of marchandisinge to the uttermost and thereby to bringe Manufactorie into your Kingdome and to set on worke all sorts of people in the realme as other nations doe, which raise theire greateness by the abundance of your native Commodities, whilest we are parlinge and disputinge whether it be good for us or not.

Maie it please your most excellent Matie[2]

I have dilligently in my travells observed how the Countries herein mentioned doe growe potent with abundance of all things to searve themselves and other Nations where nothing groweth and that their never dryed fountains of wealth by which they raise their estate to such an admirable height (as they are, at this day even a wonder to the world) proceedeth from your Ma.^{tie's} sea and land. I thus moved, began to dyve into the depth of theire policies of circumventinge practices whereby they drayne and still covet[3] to exhaust the wealth and coyne of this kingdome and soe with our own commodities to weaken us and finally beate us quite out of tradinge in other countries. I found that they more fully obteyned these theire purposes by theire con-

---

[2] The copy reprinted in the works by Oldys included in his life of Ralegh begins here as also does one copy in the Public Record Office SP 14/118 (from which therefore it appears to have been taken). The other copy in the Public Record Office begins "Observations for your most excellent Matie etc." as on the previous page.

[3] 'Cometh' in P.R.O. copy.

venient privileges and settled constitucions than England with all the laws and super abundance of homebred commodities which God hath vouchsafed your sea and land. And these and other mentioned in this booke are the urgent causes that provoked me (in my love and bounden dutie to your Matie and my countrie) to addresse my former booke to your princely hands for consideration.

By which their privilege they drawe multitudes of Marchants to trade with them and many other nations to inhabit amongst them which makes them populous, and then they make storehouses of all forraine commodities, wherewith upon every occasion of scarcytie and dearth, they are able to furnish forraine countries with plentie of these commodities which before in time of plentie they ingrossed and brought home from the same places which doth greatly augment power and treasure to their State, besides the common good in setting their people and poore on worke.

To these privileges they add smalness of custome and libertie of trade which maketh them flourish and their countries soe plentiful of all kynd of coyne and commodities (where little or nothing groweth) and their marchants soe rich that when a losse cometh they scarce feele it.

To bringe this to passe they have many advantages of us. The one is by theire fashioned shipps called Boyers, Hoyebarks, Hoyes and others that are made to holde greate bulke of marchandize and to saile with a few men for proffitt. For example, though an English shipp of 200 tonnes and a Holland shipp (or any other of the pettie states) of the same burthen, be at Danske or any other place beyond the seas (or in England) they doe searve the marchant better cheap by £100 in his frieght (than we can) by reason he hath but 9 or 10 mariners and we neere 30. Thus he saveth

20 mens meate and wages in a voyage (and so in all other theire shipps according to theire burthen) by which meanes they are fraighted wheresoever they come to greate proffitt, whilest our ships lye still and decaye, or go to Newcastle for coles.

Of this theire smalness of Custome inwardes and outwardes we have daylie experience, for if two English shipps or two of any other nation be at Bourdeaux both laden with wynes of 300 tonnes a peece the one bound for Holland or any other pettie state the other for England the marchant shall paie above 900 pounds customs here (and other duties) when the other in Holland or any other pettie state shall be cleared for less than £50. And soe in all other wares of marchandizes accordingly, which draweth all Nations to traffique with them; And although it seems but small duties which they receive, yet the multitudes of all kynde of commodities and coyne is so greate that is brought in by themselves and others, that they receave more customs and duties to the state (by the greatness of their commerce) in one yeare than England doth in two yeares. For the 100th part of commodities are not spent in Holland but vented into other countries which maketh all the countrie marchants to buy and sell and increase shipps and maryners to transport them.

My travells and meaninge is not to diminish (neither hath been) your Maties revenues but exceedingly to increase them (as shall appeare) and yet please the people as in other parts they do.

Notwithstandinge theire excises bringe them in great revenues, yet whosoever will adventure to Bordeaux but for 6 tonnes of wine, shall be free of excise in his owne house all the yeare longe; and this is done of purpose to anymate and increase Marchants in their countrie.

And if it happen that any trade be stopped by any forrain nation (which they heretofore usually had) or heare of any goode trading (which they never had) they will hynder others and seeke either by favour, money or force to open the gapp of Traffique for advancement of trade amongst themselves and imployment of their people.

And when there is a new trade or course erected, they give free Customes inwardes and outwardes for the better maintenance of Navigation and encouragement of the people to the business.

Thus they and others gleane the wealth and strength from us to themselves and these reasons followinge procureth them this advantage of us, vizt.

1. The marchant stapelers which make all things of aboundance, by reason of theire storehouses contynually replenished with all kind of commodyties.

2. The Libertie of free traffique for strangers to buy and sell in Holland and other countries and states (as if they were free borne) maketh great entercourse.

3. The small duties leavyed upon marchants draweth all nations to trade with them.

4. Theire fashioned shipps contynually freighted before ours, by reason of theire few maryners and great bulke, searving the marchant cheape.

5. Theire forwardness to further all manner of tradinge.

6. The wonderfull imployment of theire Busses for fishinge and the greate returns they make.

7. Theire giving free Custome inwardes and outwardes for any new erected trade by means whereof they have already gotten almost the sole trade into theire owne handes.

All Nations may buy and sell freely in France and there is free Custome outwardes twice or thrice in a yeare, at which tyme our marchants themselves doe make theire greate sales of English commodities and doe buy and lade theire great bulk of French commodities to searve for the whole yeare. And in Rochell in France and in Brittaine free custome all the yeare longe (except some small toll) which maketh greate traffique and maketh them flourish.

In Denmark, to incourage and inrich theire Marchants, and to increase shipps and maryners, free custome all the yeare longe for their own marchants (except one month) between Bartholomewtide and Michalmas.

The Haunce[4] Townes have advantage of·us (as Holland and other petty states have) and in most things imitate them which maketh them exceedinge riche and plentifull of all kyndes of commodities and coyne and so stronge in shipps and maryners that some of theire Townes have neere 1000 Saile of Shippes.

The Marchandises of France, Portingall, Spaine, Italy, Turkey, East and West Indies are transported most by the Hollanders and other pettie states into the East and North-east Kingdome of Pomerland, Spruceland, Poland, Denmark, Sweathen, Leifland and Germayne and the merchandize brought from the last mentioned kingdomes (being wonderfull many) are likewise by the Hollanders and other

---

[4] Hanse-Towns.

pettie states most transported into the southerne and westerne dominions and yet the situation of England lyeth far better for a storehouse to searve the southerne East and Northeast regions than theires doth, and hath far better meanes to doe it, if we will bend our course for it.

Noe sooner a dearth of fish, wyne or corne here and other marchandize but forthwith the Embdeners, Hamburgers and Hollanders out of their storehouses layde 50 or 100 shipps or more dispersing themselves rounde about this kingdome and carry away great store of coyne and wealth for little commodities in these types of dearth. By which meanes they sucke our commonwealth of theire riches, cut down our marchants and decaye our Navigation, not with their naturall commodities which growether in theire owne countries but the marchandizes of other countries and kingdomes.

Therefore it is far more easyer for us to searve our selves, hold up our marchants and increase our shipps and maryners and strengthen the kingdome and not only keepe our money in our own realme (which other nations still robbeth us of) but bringe in theires, who carryeth ours away, and make the bancke of coyne and storehouse to searve other nations as well and far better cheape than they.

Amsterdam is never without 700 thousand quarters of corne, besides the plentie they daylie vent and none of this groweth in theire own countrie. A dearth in England, France, Spain, Italy, Portingall and other places is truly obsearved to inrich Holland 7 yeares after and likewise the petty states.

For example, the last dearth sixe yeares past (about November 1614)[5] the Hamburgers, Embdeners and Hollanders out of their own storehouses furnished this kingdome and from Southampton, Exiter and Bristow, in a year and a halfe they carryed away neere 200 thousande poundes from these 3 ports only. Then what greate quantities of Coynes was transported round about your kingdome from every porte towne and from the citie of London and other cities cannot be esteemed so little as 2 millions, to the great decay of your kingdome, impoverishing the people, discredit to the companie of Marchants and dishonour to the lande; that any Nation that have no corne in theire own countrie growing should searve this famous kingdome which God hath so inabled within itself.

They have a contynuall trade into this kingdome with 5 or 600 shipps yearly with marchandizes of other countries and kingdomes and store them up in storehouses here untill the price rise to theire myndes and we trade not with 50 shipps into theire countries in a yeare and the sayd number are about this realme every easterly wynde for the most part to lade coles and other marchandise.

Unless there be a scarcytie and dearth or high prices, all marchants doe forbeare that place where greate impositions are layed upon the marchandise and those places slenderly shipped ill searved and at deare rates and often tymes in

---

[5] The comment in parenthesis was entered in the margin in this copy and is not in the same writing as that of the body of the treatise. It appears to refer to the last dearth as of November 1614 but in fact that was not a period of high prices but falling prices. The last dearth six years past was more probably in 1608 when in the last months wheat prices were at famine levels. See *History of Agriculture and Prices in England* by James E. Thorold Rogers, Volume V, 1583-1702. Pp. 186-189 (Reprint 1963). The reference may be to the date of the pamphlet.

scarcytie and want imployment for the people. And these pettie states finding truly by experience that small duties imposed upon marchandise draweth all traffique until them and free liberty for strangers to buy and sell doth make contynuall marte. Therefore what excises or impositions are layed upon the common people, yet they still ease, upholde and maintayne the marchants by all possible meanes, of purpose to drawe the wealth and strength of Christendome to themselves, whereby it appeareth though the duties be but small yet the customs for goinge out and cominge in doth soe abounde that they increase theire revenues greatly and make proffitt plentie and imployment of all sortes by sea and lande to searve themselves and other nations as is admirable to beholde. And likewise the greate concourse which groweth by the same meanes enableth the common people to beare theire burthen layd upon them and yet they growe rich by reason of the greate commerce and trade occasioned by their convenyent privileges and commodious constitutions.

There was an entercourse of traffique in Genoa and there was the flower of Commerce as appeareth by theire anciente recordes and their sumptuous buildings (for all nations traded with marchandise to them) and there was the store-house of all Italye and other places. But after they had sett a greate custome of 16 per cent all nations left tradinge with them which made them give themselves wholly to usury, and at this day we have not 3 shipps goe thether in a yeare. But to the contrary, the Duke of Florence builded Ligorne[6] and set small custome upon marchandise and gave them greate and pleasinge privileges which hath made a rich and stronge cyttie with a flourishing state.

[6] Leghorn.

Furthermore touching some particulars needeful to be considered of the mightie hudge rich fishing that every could be heard of in the world is upon the coast of England, Scotland and Ireland. But the greate fishing is in the low Countries and other pettie states wherewith they searve themselves and all Christendome as shall appear.

In fower townes in the east kingdomes within the Sownd, Quinsbrough Elbing Statten and Dansicke there is carryed and vented in a yeare between 30 or 40 thousand lasts of Herrings, sold but at 15 or 16 pounds per last, is about 620,000 pounds and we none.

Besides Denmarke, Norwaie, Sweathen,[7] Leifland, Rie, Revelle,[8] the Narve and other porte townes within the Sounde, there is carried and vented about 10 thousand laste of herrings, sold at 15 or 16 pounds the last, is 170,000 poundes more yearly: in such request are our herringe there, that they are of ten tymes sold for 20, 24, 30 and 36 pounds the last. And we send not one barrell into all those East countries.

The Hollanders sent into Russia neere 15 hundred laste of Herrings sold about 30 shilling the barrell, is 27,000 poundes. And we but about 20 or 30 lasts. To Stoade, Hambrough, Breame[9] and Embden upon the river of Elue, Weazer and Embs, is carried and vented of Fish and Herrings about 6,000 lasts, solde but about 16 or 16 poundes the last, is 100,000 poundes and we none.

Cleaveland, Gulickland, up the river of Rhine to Cullan, Franchford on the Maine and so over all Germanie, is carryed and vented of Fish and herrings neere 22 thousand

---

[7] Sweden.
[8] Neville in McCulloch.
[9] Bremen.

lasts, sold but at 20 pounds the last, is 440,000 pounds and we none.

Up the river of Maze, Leige, Mastrith,[10] Vendlow, Zutphen, Deventer, Campen, Swoole[11] and all over Lukeland is carried and vented 7,000 lasts of herrings, sold at 20 pounds the last, is 140,000 poundes and we none.

To Gelderland, Artois, Henault, Brabant, Flanders, up the river of Antwerpe, all over the Archduke's Countries is carried and vented between 8 or 9 thousand lasts sold at 18 poundes the last, is 171,000 poundes and we none.

The Hollanders and others carryed of all sorte of herringe to Roane only in one yeare: besides all other parts of France 5,000 lasts of Herrings sould at 20 poundes the last, is 100,000 poundes. And we not 100 laste thether. They are sold often tymes there for 13, 23 and 30 poundes the laste.

Between Christmas and Lent the duties for Fish and Herrings come to 15,000 crownes at Roane, only the year the late queene deceased (Sir Thomas Parry, was agent there then and St. Saviours his man knows it to be true, who handled the business for pullinge downe the impositions) then what greate somes of money came to call the Porte townes to inrich the French king's coffers and to all the kings and states throughout Christendome to inrich theire coffers, besides the great quantity vented to the straights and the multitude spent in the low Countries, where there is likewise sold for many 100,000 poundes more yearly, is necessaries to be remembered and the streame to be turned to the good of this kingdome, to whose sea coastes only God hath sent and given these great blessings and multitudes

---

[10] Mastrecht.
[11] Zwolle.

of riches for us to take, howsoever it hath beene neglected to the hurte of this kingdome. That any nation should carry away out of this realme yearely greate masses of money for fish they take in our seas, and solde againe by them to us, which must needes be a greate dishonour to this nation and hyndrance to this realme.

From any porte towne of any kingdome in Christendome the Bridgmaister or the wharfe maister for 20 shillings a year will deliver a true noate of the number of lasts of herrings brought to their wharfes and their prices commonly they are sold at. But the number brought to Dansick, Cullen, Rotterdam and Enchusen is soe greate as it will cost 3, 4 or 5 poundes for a true noate.

The abundance of corne groweth in the East Kingdomes. But the greate storehouses for Grayne to searve Christendome and the heathen countries in tyme of dearth is in the low Countries wherewith upon every occasion of scarcytie and dearth, they do inrich themselves 7 yeares later, imploye their people and get greate freights for theire shippes in other countries and we not one in that course.

The mightie Vynniards and store of salte is in France and Spain but the greate vyntage and staple of salte is in the Lowe countries and they send neere 1000 saile of shippes with salte and wyne only into the east kingdomes yearely, besides many other places. And we not one in that course.

The exceedinge groves of wood are in the East kingdomes. But the hudge piles of waynscotts clapboardes, fir deale, masts and Tymber, is in the low Countries where none groweth, whereas they searve themselves and other parts, and this kingdome with these commodities; they have 5 or 600 greate longe shipps contynually using that trade. And we none in that course.

The woolle, cloth, leade, Tynne and dyvers other commodities are in England. But by means of our wool and cloth going out rough, undressed and undyed, there is an exceeding manufactories and draperie in the low Countries, wherewith they searve themselves and other nations which advanceth greatly the imployment of theire people at home and traffique abroad, and putteth downe ours in forraine parts where our marchants trade unto with our owne commodities.

We send into the East kingdomes yearely but 100 shipps and our trade chiefly dependeth upon 3 townes, Elbinge, Kingsborough and Dansicke for making our sales and buyinge theire commodities sent into this realme at deere rates which this kingdome beareth the burden of.

The Lowe Countries send into the East kingdomes yearely about 3,000 shipps tradinge into every Cyttie and Porte Towne taking the advantage and venting their commodities to exceedinge profit and buying and ladinge theire shippes with plentie of those commodities which they have from every of those Townes 20 per cent better cheape than we, by reason of the difference of the coyne and theire fish yieldeth reddy money which greatly advanceth theire traffique and decayeth ours.

They send into France, Spaine, Portingall and Italy from the East kingdomes (that passeth through the Sound and through your narrow Seas) yearely of the East countrie commodities about 2,000 shippes and we none in the Course.

They trade into all Cities and Porte Townes in France and we chiefly to 5 or 6.

They traffique into every Cittie and Porte towne round about this lande with 5 or 600 shipps yeerely and we chiefly but to 3 townes in theire countries and but with 40 shipps.

Notwithstanding the Low Countries have as many shipps and vessels as all kingdomes of Christendome have (let England be one) and build every yeere neere 1000 ships and not a tymber tree growing in theire own countrie and that alsoe all theire home bred commodities that growe in theire lande in a yeare lesse than 100 good shipps are able to carry them away at one tyme, yet they handle the matter soe (for setting them all on worke) that theire traffique with the Haunce Townes exceedeth in shipping all Christendome.

We have all things of our owne in superabundance to increase traffique and tymber to build shipps and commodities of our owne to lade about 1000 shipps and vessels at one tyme (besides the greate fishing) and as fast as they have made theire voyage might relade againe and soe yeare after yeare all the yeare longe to contynue: yet our shipps and maryners declyne and traffique and marchants daylie decaye.

The mayne bulke and masse of herrings from whence they raise so many millions yearely that inrich other kingdomes kings and states coffers and likewise theire owne people proceedeth from our seas and lands and the retourne of the commodities and coyne they bringe home in exchange of Fish and other commodities are soe hudge as would require a large discourse aparte. All the amendes they make us is that they beate us out of trade in all parts with our own commodities.

For instance we had a greate trade in Russia 70 yeares and about 14 yeares past we sent store of goodly shipps to trade into those parts and 3 yeares past we set out but 4 and this last yeare 2 or 3. But to the contrarie the Hollanders about 20 yeares since traded thether with 2 shipps only, yet now they are increased to about 30 or 40 and one of these shipps is as greate as 2 of ours and the same tyme (in theire troubles there) that we decreased, they increased and the chiefest commodities they carry with thether is English cloth, herrings taken on our coast, English leade and Pewter made of our tynne, besides other commodities all which we may doe better than they. And although it be a Cheape countrie and the trade very gainefull yet we have almost brought it to nought by disorderly tradinge, joynt stocke and the marchants bandinge themselves one against another.

And soe likewise we used to have 8 or 9 shipps to goe contynually a fishinge to Wardehouse and this yeare but one and soe per rato they outgoe us in all kinde of fishinge and marchandisinge in all countries by reason they spare noe cost, nor denye no priviledges that may incourage advancement of trade and manufacture.

Now if it please and stand with your Majesties good likinge

To take notice of these things which I have conceaved to be fitt for your Maties consideration, which (in all humbleness as Duttie byndeth me) I doe tender unto your Matie for the unfayned zeale I beare to the advancement of your honour and proffit and the general good of all your subjects: It being apparent that noe 3 kingdomes in Christendome can compaire with your Matie for support of traffique and contynuall imployment of your people (within themselves) having soe greate meanes inlarge your traffique, make your kingdome powerful and your people riche; yet through idleness they are pore, wantinge imployment, many of your land and coast townes much rewinated and your kingdome in need of coyne, your shippinge, traffique and maryners decayed. Whilest your Maties neighboure princes (without these meanes) abound in wealth, inlarge their townes, increase their shippinge, traffique and maryners and fynd out such imployment for theire people that they are all advantages to their common wealth. Only by ordayning commodious constitutions in marchandising and fullness of trade to all theire people in manufactorie.

God hath blest your Ma.tie with incomparable benefits

As with copper, Leade, Iron, Tynne, Allome, copperas, saffron, fells and dyvers other native commodities of the number of 100 and other manufactories vendable to the number of about 1000 (as shall appeare) besides corne, whereof greate quantytie of Beere is made and most transported by strangers as alsoe Wooll, whereof much is shipped forth unwrought into Cloth or Stuffes and Cloth transported undressed and undyed which doth imploye and maintayne neere 50,000 people, in forriagn parts, your Ma.ties owne people wanting the imployment in England, many of them being inforced to live in greate wante and seeke it beyond the seas.

Coles which doth imploye neere 600 strangers shippes yeerely to transport them out of this kingdome whilst we do not imply 20 ships in that course.

Iron ordnance which is a jewell of greate value, far more than it is accompted, by reason that no other countries could ever attayne unto it (although they have assayed it with great charge).

Your Ma.tie hath timber of your owne for building of shipps and commodities plentie to lade them which commodities other nations want. Yet your Ma.ties people decline in shipping, traffique and maryners.

These inconveniences happen by three causes especially.

1. The unprofitable course of marchandisinge.
2. For want of the true course of full manufactorie of our home bred commodities.

3. By under valueinge of our coynes, contrary to the role of other nations.

For instance

The marchant Adventurer by over tradinge upon credit or with money taken upp upon exchange, whereby they loose usually 10 or 12 and sometimes 15 or 16 per cent, are inforced to make sale of theire clothes at under rates to keepe theire Creditt, whereby cloth (being the jewell of the land) is under valued and the marchant in shorte tyme eaten out.

The marchants of Ipswich whose trade for Elbinge is chiefly for fine clothes and some few sortinge clothes all dyed and dressed within your land doe for the most parte buy their fine clothes upon tyme and by reason they goe so much upon creditt they are inforced (not being able to stand upon their marketts) to sell, giving 15 or 18 months day of payment for theire clothes, and havinge solde them, they then presently sell theire bills (soe taken for Cloth) allowinge after the rate of 14 or 15 and some tymes 20 per cent which money they imploye forthwith in wares at excessive prices and lose as much money that way by that tyme theire wares be solde at home. Thus by over runninge themselves upon creditt, they disable themselves and others, inhauncing the price of forrain commodities and pulling down the rates of our owne.

The West Country marchants that trade with clothes into France or Spain, doe usually imploye theire servants (young men of small experience) who by cunning combyninge of the French and Spanish marchants are so intrapped that when all customs and charges be accoumpted, theire masters shall hardly receive their principall money. As for returns out of France, theire Silver and Golde is soe heighe rated, that our marchants cannot bring it home but to greate losse. Therefore the French marchants set heigher rates of theire commodities which we must either buy deere or let our money lye dead there a longe tyme, until we may conveniently imploye the same.

The Northern marchants of Yorke, Hull and Newcastle trade only in white kersies and cullored dozens and every marchant (be his adventure never soe small) doth for the most parte send over an unexperienced youth unfitt for marchandisinge which bringeth to the stranger greater advantage but to his maister and common weale great hyndrance. For they before theire goodes be landed, goe to the stranger and buy such quantities of Iron, Flax, Corne and other commodities as they are bounde to lade their shipps with all, which shipps they ingage themselves to relade within three weeks or a month and doe give the price the marchant stranger asketh, because he gives them credit and lets them ship away theire Iron, Flax and other commodities before they have sold theire kersies and other clothes. By which meanes extraordinarie deere commodities are returned into the Realme and the servant also inforced to sell his clothes under foote and often tymes to losse to keepe his creditt and to make payment, for the goodes before shipped home, having some 20 daies or a months respitt, to sell the clothes and to give the marchant satisfaction for his Iron, Flax and other wares. By which extremities our home bred commodities are abased.

Touching Manufacture

There have beene about 80 thousand undrest undyed clothes yearly transported.[12]

---

[12] In Public Record Office copy, a note in the margin says: "I am able to prove this if need require."

It is therefore evident that the kingdome hath been yearley deprived of about 400 thousand poundes which in this 55 years is neere 20 millions that would have beene gayned by the labour of poore workmen in that tyme, with the marchantes gaines for bringinge in dyinge stuffs, and returns of clothes dressed and dyed with other benefits to the realme besides exceedinge inlargeing of traffique and increase of shipps and maryners.

There would have been gayned in that tyme about 3 million by increase of Custome upon commodities returned for clothes dressed and dyed and for dyinge stuffes which could have more plentifully beene brought in and used for the same. (It is to be supposed that Kinge Phillipp knew well what he did in procuring the first licence of white and undressed clothes into the Lowe Countries in Q. Maries tyme.)[13]

There have beene also transported in that tyme yearly by Bayse, Northern and Devonshire Kersies white, about 50 thousand clothes coumpting three kersies to a cloth, whereby hath beene lost about 5 millions by those sortes of Clothes in that tyme which would have gone to poore workmen for theire labour, with the Custome for dyinge stuffs and the people's proffitt for bringing them in with retornes of other commodities.

Bayes are transported white unto Amsterdam and being there dressed and dyed, are shipped in to Spain, Portingall and other Kingdomes where they are sold in the name of Flemish bayes, settinge theire own towne seale upon them;

---

[13] In the Public Record Office copy this comment by another hand appears in the margin. Actually the Merchant Adventurers secured a license to send out 30,000 undressed and undyed cloths in 1564.

soe that we lose the very name of our home bred commodities and other countries get the reputation and proffitt thereof. Lamentable it is that this land should be deprived of soe many of the above mentioned millions and that our native commodities of clothes (ordayned by God for the natural subjects) beinge so royall and rich in itself, should be driven to soe small advantage of reputation and proffitt to your Ma.tie and people and soe much improved and intercepted by strangers. Consideringe that God hath enable and given your Ma.tie power to advance dressing and dyinge and transportinge of all your clothes within a year or two, I speeke it knowingley, to show how it may be done laudably, lawfully and approved to be honorable, feasable and proffitable.

All the companies of your lande transporte their clothes dressed and dyed, to the good of your kingdome (except the Marchant Adventurers) whereby the Easterland and Turkey marchants (with other Companies) do increase your Ma.ties Customes by bringing in and spendinge dyinge stuffs and setting your people on worke by dressing and dyinge affore transportation and they might increase far more custome to your Ma.tie and make much more proffitt to themselves and this realme and set many thousands of poore people more on worke for dressing and dyinge and likewise imploye more shipps and maryners for bringing in dying stuffs, were it not for the Marchant Adventurers who transporte theire clothes white, roughe, undrest and undyed into the Low Countries where they sell them to the marchant strangers who afterwards dress, dye and stretch them to such unreasonable lengths (contrarie to our Law) that they prevent and forestall our Marketts and cross the just prohibitions of our State and Realme by theire Agents or Factors lyinge in dyvers places with our owne clothes to the great decaye of this kingdome in generall and discreditt of our clothes in particular.

If the accompte were truly knowne, it would be founde that they make not cleere proffitt (only by clothe transported rough, undressed and undyed) 60,000 poundes a year. But it is most apparent that your Matie in your customes, your marchants in theire sales and prices, your subjects in theire Labours (for lacke of not dressing and dyinge) your shipps and maryners in not bringing in of dyinge stuffs and spending of Allome, is hyndered yearly neere a million of pounds. So that Trade is dryven to the great hyndrance of your Matie and people, by permitting your Native Commodities to passe rough, undressed and undyed by the Marchant Adventurers.

Touching Fishinge

The great sea business if Fishinge doth imploye neere 20,000 shipps and vessels and 400,000 people are imployed yeerly upon your Coasts of England, Scotland and Ireland with 60 ships of warr which may prove dangerous.

The Hollanders only have about 3000 shipps to fish with all and 50,000 people are imployed yeerely by them upon your Maties Coasts of England, Scotland and Ireland. These 3000 fishing shipps and vessels of the Hollanders doth imploye neere 9000 other shipps and vessels and 150,000 persons more by sea and land to make provision to dress and transporte the fish they take and returne commodities, whereby they are inabled and do build yeerely 1000 shipps and vessels, havinage not one tymber tree growing in theire own countries nor home bred Commodities to layde 100 shipps and yet they have 20,000 shipps and vessels and all imployed.

King Henry the Seventh desyrous to make his kingdomes powerfull and rich by increase of shipps and maryners and imployment of his people sent unto his sea coast townes, movinge them to sett upp the great and rich fishinge with promise to give them needefull priviledges and to furnish them with Loanes of money (if need ware) to incourage them. Yet his people were slacke. Now since I have traced this business and made my endeavours knowne unto your Matie your Noblemen, Able merchants and others who (havinge set downe under theire handes for more assurance) promise to disburge large somes of money for the building up of this great and riche large Sea Cittie which will increase more strength to your hande, give more Comforte and doe more good to all your Citties and townes than all the Companies of your kingdome having fitt and needeful priviledges for the upholdinge and strengtheninge of soe waightie and behoofefull a business.

For example, 20 busses built and put into a Sea Coast towne where there is not one shipp before, there must be to carry, recarry, transport and make provision for one Busse three shipps. Likewise every shipp setteth on work 30 several trades and occupations and 400 persons by Sea and land in soe much as 300 persons are not able to make one fleete of netts in 4 months for one Busse which is no small imployment.

Thus by 20 busses are sett on work neere 8000 persons by sea and land and an increase of about 1000 maryners, and a fleet of 80 saile of shipps to belonge to one towne where none ware before, to take the wealth out of the sea, to inriche and strengthen the land, only by the raisinge of 20 busses.

Then what good 1000 or 2000 will doe, I leave unto your Ma.ties consideration.

It is worthy to be noated how necessarie fishermen are to the Common Wealth and how needeful to be advanced and cherrished, vizt.

1. For takinge Gods blessing out of the sea, to inrich the realme which otherwise we lose.

2. For setting the people on worke.

3. For making plentie and cheapness in the realm.

4. For increasinge of shipping to worke the land powerfull.

5. For a contynuall nursery for breadinge and increasinge our maryners.

6. For making imployment of all sortes of people as blynde, lame and others by sea and land from 10 or 12 yeeres upwardes.

7. For inriching your Ma.ties coffers for marchandises returned from other countries for fish and herringes.

8. For the increase and inablinge of Marchants which now droope and daylie decaye.

Touching Coyne

For the most parte all monarches and free states (both heathen and Christian) as Turkey, Barbary, France, Poland and others, to holde for a generall rule of never faylinge proffitt, to keep their coyne at higher rates within their own territories than it is in other kingdomes.

The Causes

1. To preserve the Coyne within their owne Territories.

2. To bringe unto themselves the Coyne of forraine princes.

3. To inforce Marchant strangers to take theire commodities at high rates which this kingdome beareth the burden of.

For Instance

The King of Barbary perceavinge the trade of Christian marchants to increase in his kingdome and that the Returns out of his Kingdome was made in Gold whereby it was most inhaunced, raised his Duckett (being then current for three ounces) to 4, 5 and 6 ounces, never the lesse it was noe more worth in England (being so raised) than when it went for 3 ounces.

This Duckett current for 3 ounces in Barbary was then worthe in England 7/6 and no more worth being raised to 6 ounces. Since which time (adding to it a small piece of gold) he hath raised it to 8 and lastly to 10 ounces. Yet at this day it is worth but 10 shillings and one penny, notwithstandinge your Maties late raising of your golde.[14]

Having thus raised his Golde, he then devised to have plentie of silver brought into his kingdome, raised the Royall of 8, being but 2 ounces current to 3 and 3 pence half penny

---

[14] In May 1611 the proclamation against the export of specie was renewed. The Privy Council gave much consideration to the desirability of raising the denomination of the coinage and finally agreed. In November 1611 the value of all gold coins was raised 10 per cent. Ralegh had agreed in favour of this. See W. A. Shaw. *The History of Currency*. P. 135. It is tempting to speculate that Keymer influenced Ralegh's observations.

which caused great plentie of silver to be brought in and to continue in his kingdome.

France

The English Jacobus goeth for 23 shillings in marchandisinge. The French crown for 7/6. Alsoe the king hath raised his silver 4 Souce in the Crowne.

North Holland

The double Jacobus goeth for 23 shillings sterling. The English shilling is there 11 styvers which is 2 shillings more in the pound.

Poland

The King of Poland raised his Hungarie Duckett from 56 to 77½ Polinsh groshes and the Reich dollar from 36 to 47½ groshes. The reich dollar worth in Poland 47½ groshes is by accoumpt valued at 6/4 starlinge and heere in England worth but 4/7. The Hungarie Duckett is worthe by accoumpt in Poland 10/4 and in England is worth but 7/10.

The Jacobus of England here current for 22 shillings. In Poland 24 shillings, at the rate of 7/10 for the Hungarie Duckett.

Now to turne the streame of riches (raised by your Maties native commodities) into the naturall channell from whence it hath been a long tyme dyverted.

Maie it please your Matie to consider these points followinge

1. Whether it be not fitt that a state marchant be settled within your Dominions which may both dispose more proffitable of the riches thereof and encoumpter pollicies of Marchant strangers who now go beyond us in all kynds of proffitable marchandisinge. (I desire that the name of State marchant be not mistaken for it shall give most ample contentment to all men.) [15]

2. Whether it be not necessaries that your native commodities should receave their full manufactories by your subjects within your dominions.

3. Whether it be not necessaries that the great sea business of fishinge be forthwithe sett forwarde.

4. Whether it be not fitt that Coles should yeilde your Ma.tie and subjects a better value by permitting them to passe out of the lande and that they be in your subjects shipping only transported.

5. Whether it be not fitt your Ma.tie presently raise your Coyne to as highe rates as it is in the parts beyond the Seas.

If it please your Ma.tie to approve of these considerations and accordingly to put them in a right course of execution, I assure myself (by God's helpe) in short tyme, your Ma.ties Customes and the contynuall cominge in to your Coffers will be exceedingly increased, your shipps and Maryners trebled, your land and wayst townes (which are now run out of gates) better replenished and your people imployed

---

[15] The comment in parenthesis appears in the margin in the Public Record Office MS.

to the greate inrichinge and honour of your kingdom (with the applause) and to the comforte of all your loyall subjects.

May it please your Matie

I have the rather undergone the paines to looke into their policies because I have heard them profess they hoped to get the whole trade and shipping of Christendome into their handes, as well for Transportations as otherwise, for the command and maistery of the seas. To which end I finde they doe daily increase their traffique augmentinge their shippinge, multiplyinge their maryners, strength and wealth in all kyndes. Whereat I have grieved the more when I consider how God hath endued this kingdome above any 3 kingdomes in Christendome with dyvers varieties of home bred commodities which others have not and cannot want and endued us with sundry other meanes to contynue and maintayne our trade of marchandizinge and fishinge beyond them all, whereby we might prevent the deceavers, ingross the commodities of the ingrossers, inriche ourselves and increase our Navigation, shipping and maryners soe as it would make all nations to vaile the Bonnet to England if we would not be still wantinge to ourselves in imployment of our people.

Which people beinge now divided into 3 parts, 2 parts of them are meere spenders and consumers of a Common Wealth. Therefore I ayme at these poynts followinge:

To allure and incourage the people for their private gayne to be all workers and erectors of a Commonwealth.

To enriche and fill your Maties Coffers by a contynuall coming in and make your people wealthy by means of theire greate and profitable tradinge and imployment.

To vente our homebred commodities to far more reputation and much more proffitt to the King and marchants of the Kingdome.

To return the marchandises of other countries at far cheaper rates than now they are. To the greate goode of the Realme in generall.

To make the land powerfull by increasinge and multiplying of shipps and maryners.

To make your peoples takinge in generall to be muche more every day than now they are which (by God's helpe) will growe continually more and more, by the great concourse and commerce that will come by settled constitutions and convenient privileges as in other parts they do, by this their great freedom of Trade.

All this and much more is done in other countries (where nothinge groweth) soe that of nothinge they make great things.

Then how muche more mightie things might we make, where so greate aboundance and varieties of homebred commodities and rich materials growes for your people to work upon and other plentifull meanes to do it withall which other nations neither have nor cannot want but (of necessitie) must be furnished from hence. And now whereas our Marchandisinge is wyld, utterly confused and out of frame (as now appeareth) a State Marchant will roundly and effectually bring all the premises to pass, fill your harbers with shipps, those shipps with maryners, your kingdom full of marchants, theire houses full of outlandish commodities and your Coffers full of Coyne (as in other parts they doe) and your people shall have just cause to holde in happie memorie that your Ma.tie was the beginner of soe proffitable praiseworthie and renoued a worke. Being the true Philosopher Stone to make your Matie a rich and potent king and your subjects happie people, only by settlinge of a State Marchant whereby your people may have fullness of trade and manufactorie. And yet holde both honorable and proffitable government without breakinge of Companies.

And for that in the settling of soe weightie a business, many things of great consequence must necessarilie fall into consideration, I humbly pray that your Matie would be pleased (for the bringing of this great service to light) to give me leave to nominate the commissioners and your Matie to give them power to call before them such men as they shall think fitt to examine and conferr with upon oath. Or otherwise as occasion shall offer: That the said Commissioners (with all speed) for the better advancement of this honorable and proffitable work may prepare and report the same to your Matie.[16]

Your Maties most loyall and true hearted subject.

John Keymer

---

[16] This paragraph does not appear in the Public Record Office copy.